My Holiday Diary

Jason Telford

Acknowledgements

Photos
All photographs, Rod Theodorou. Layout photography, Rupert Horrox.

Illustrations
Oxford Illustrators, page 5; page 7; page 9, right; page 17, bottom.
All other illustrations by Jason Telford.

Map on pages 12 and 13 copyright of Sea World, Florida.

Special thanks to Jason Telford.

Heinemann Educational Publishers
Halley Court, Jordan Hill, Oxford OX2 8EJ
a division of Reed Educational & Professional Publishing Ltd

OXFORD FLORENCE PRAGUE MADRID ATHENS
MELBOURNE AUCKLAND KUALA LUMPUR SINGAPORE TOKYO
IBADAN NAIROBI KAMPALA JOHANNESBURG GABORONE
PORTSMOUTH NH (USA) CHICAGO MEXICO CITY SAO PAULO

© Reed Educational & Professional Publishing Ltd 1997

First published 1997

02 01 00 99 98

10 9 8 7 6 5 4 3 2

British Library Cataloguing in Publication Data
A catalogue record for this book is available from the British Library.

ISBN 0 435 09569 2   *My Holiday Diary* individual copy pack:
                        6 copies of 1 title

ISBN 0 435 09416 5   Stage F pack: 1 each of 7 titles

All rights reserved. No part of this publication may be reproduced or transmitted in any form by any means, electronic or mechanical, including photocopy, recording or any information storage and retrieval system without permission in writing from the publishers.

Colour reproduction by Reacta Graphics.

Printed and bound in Great Britain by Scotprint.

Contents

Going on holiday 4
We arrive 6
At the beach 8
Collecting shells 10
Sea World 12
Killer whale 14
Back at the hotel 16
Shark tooth beach 18
Going home 20
My holiday highlights 21
Make your own holiday diary 22
Index 24

Sunday 5th August
Going on holiday

Woke up at 5.30a.m. We're off to America! After driving for two hours we arrived at the airport. We walked down a long corridor then on to the plane. TAKE OFF!

↑ This is me!

↑ My sister Lydia

This was my first trip on a plane! It had lots of TVs hanging from the ceiling.

Florida—
the Sunshine State

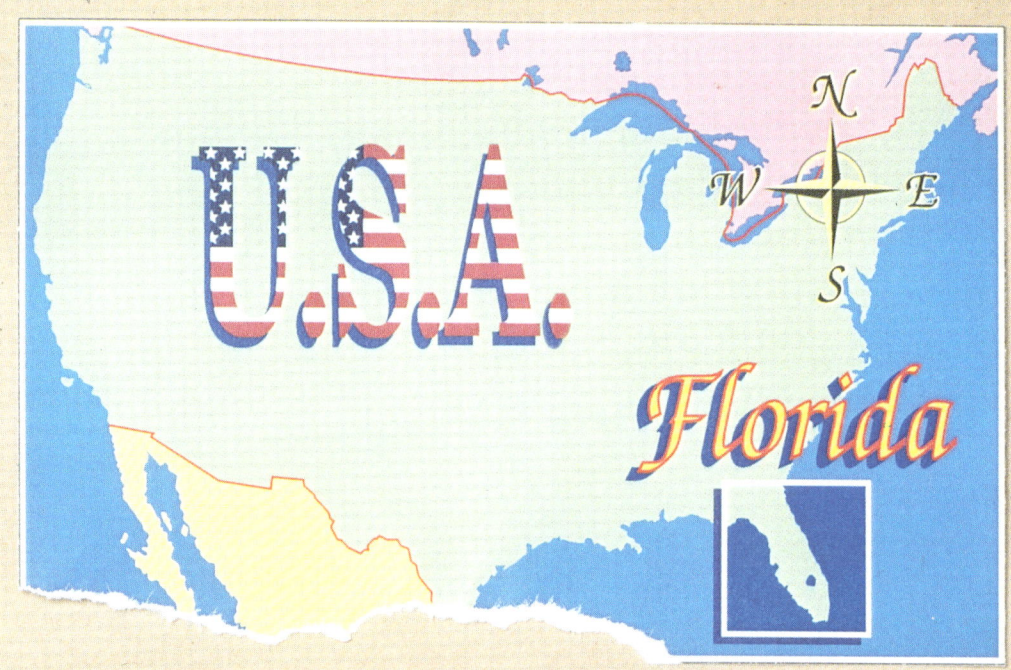

It was boring on the plane. We had to sit for hours and hours. At last we landed in Florida! It was cloudy. Mum said, 'Where's the sun?'

We arrive

We drove for hours to our hotel in Sarasota. It has a swimming pool but Mum said we couldn't go in. Mum and Dad were grumpy. Holidays are supposed to be fun!

Alligator letter box

A Florida car number plate. What's a manatee?

At the hotel

The swimming pool

Monday 6th August

Lydia woke up at 4.00a.m.
Mum and Dad were angry with her!
Had breakfast in the hotel.
Then we went into the pool.
It was really hot and sunny so
Mum and Dad were happy!

By the swimming pool

Mum and Dad — I took this photo!

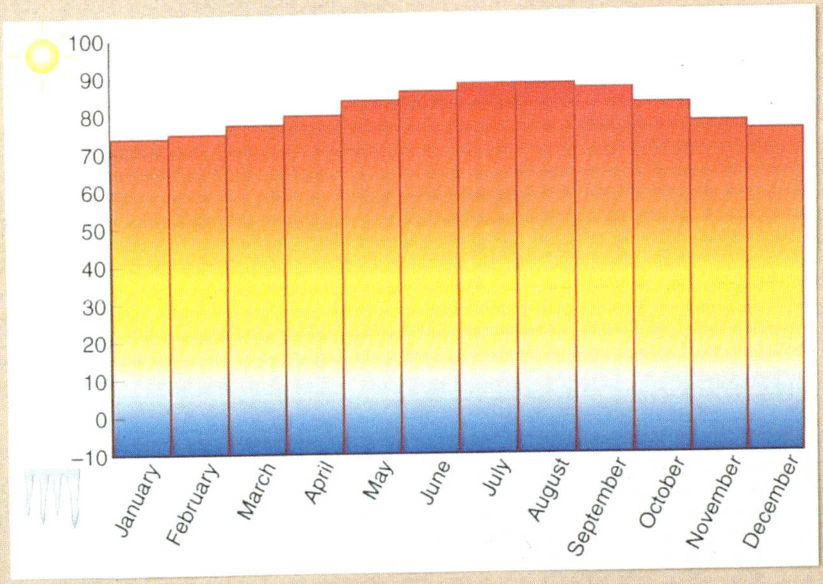

It's hot in August!

At the beach

We went to the beach.
Lydia and I made a big fort.
I cut my foot on a shell.
Dad put a plaster on it.

I wonder what made these footprints?

We saw a green flag flying on the beach. I asked a lifeguard what the flags mean. This is what they mean.

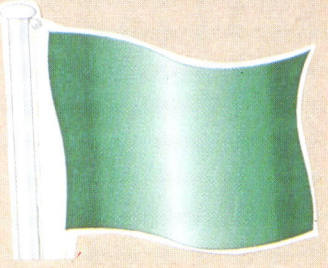

OK to swim

Mum the lifeguard!

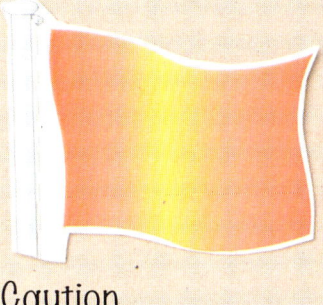

Caution

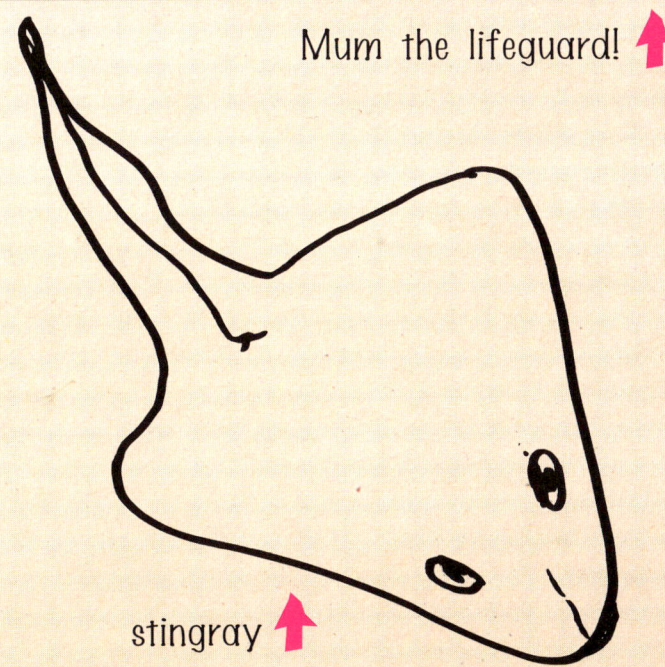

stingray

Danger! Don't swim!

Dangerous marine life — jellyfish, stingrays or sharks!

Collecting shells

↑ Looking for shells

There were lots of shells on the beach. Lydia and I collected about 100 shells but Mum said we couldn't take them with us. Mum took a photo of our shells.

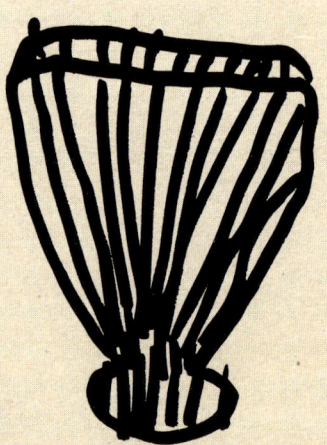

Tuesday 7th August
Sea World

Woke up at 6.00a.m. Drove to Orlando to Sea World. Lydia felt sick in the car. She gets too excited.

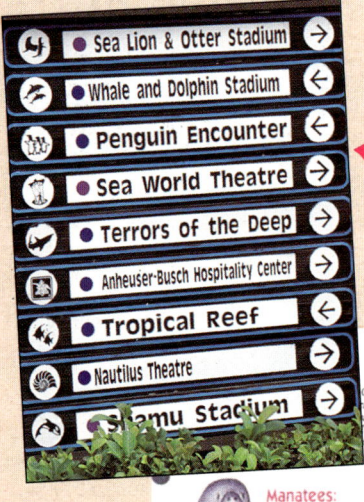

There's lots to see at Sea World!

We saw sharks and touched some stingrays, but they didn't sting us. At last I found out what a manatee is. They are nearly extinct. Sea World rescues injured manatees.

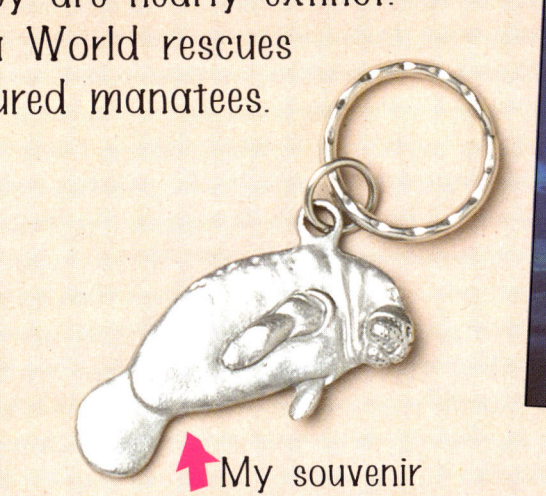
⬆ My souvenir

⬆ A manatee — very fat!

I was allowed to feed fish to the dolphins. ⬇

Killer whale

Warning!

We went to see Shamu the orca.
Orcas are killer whales.
They are not dangerous.
The trainers swim with them.

Shamu under the water

This is us watching Shamu.

Wow! Look out for splashes!

Splash!

Shamu is BIG!
The trainers asked a man to stand by the pool. Then Shamu splashed him!
We drove back to the hotel. What a great day!

The trainers feed fish to Shamu.

Wednesday 8th August

Back at the hotel

We stayed at the hotel because Mum and Dad were tired. Lydia and I swam in the pool. We met some other kids and we played with them.

Me in the swimming pool

A palm tree near the hotel

When it was dark Mum and Dad took us to a restaurant. I had a pizza. Lydia had shrimps. Yuk! I got bitten by millions of mosquitoes.

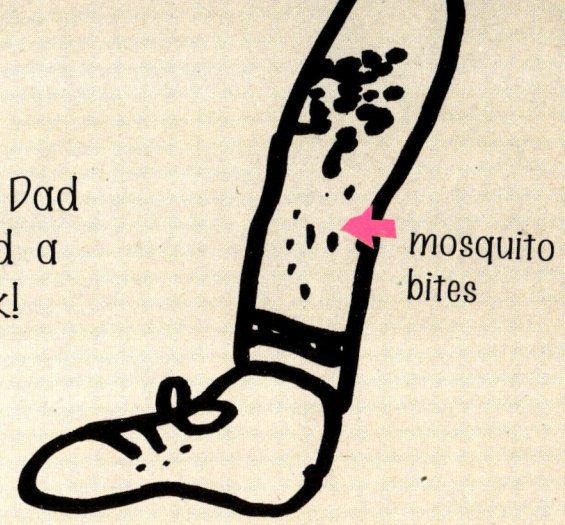

mosquito bites

KID'S FOOD
A SPECIAL MENU FOR CHILDREN 12 AND UNDER

BREAKFAST
Served 6:30 AM to 11:00 AM

FLUFF 'N' STUFF
Scrambled egg, two slices of bacon,
buttered toast and jelly............................$2.95

SILVER DOLLARS
Five silver dollar pancakes, two slices of bacon,
whipped butter and hot maple syrup.............$2.95

FRENCH TOAST 'N BACON
Thick sliced bread, dipped in our special batter,
served golden brown with two slices of bacon...$2.95

MINI OMELETTE
Fluffy two egg omelette, with American cheese
served with bacon and hash browns..............$3.50

LUNCH OR DINNER
Served 11:00 AM to Closing

PEANUT BUTTER AND JELLY.........................$2.95
GRILLED CHEESE SANDWICH.........................$2.95
SHRIMP BASKET W/FRENCH FRIES...................$4.95
QUARTER POUND HOT DOG
served with fries and pickle spear..................$3.50
BEEF BURGER $3.95   OR   CHEESE BURGER $4.25
A quarter pound of lean beef on a toasted
bun with fries and pickle spear
FRIED CHICKEN FINGERS (4)
served with fries and pickle spear..................$4.50
5" Cheese or Pepperoni Pizza.......................$3.95

BEVERAGES

Soda Pop..............95¢   Hot Chocolate..............95¢
Glass of Milk..........95¢   Juice (Apple or Orange)....95¢
Chocolate Milk.......$1.00   Shirley Temple............$1.50

All prices are subject to 7% Florida State Tax

Thursday 9th August
Shark tooth beach

Went to Venice Beach. This is a famous beach where you can find real sharks' teeth in the sand!

Looking for sharks' teeth ➡

No luck yet!

We looked in the sand for ages! We found 12 sharks' teeth. The teeth are fossils. Fossils are millions of years old! Dad got a guide book all about sharks' teeth.

Give me back my teeth!

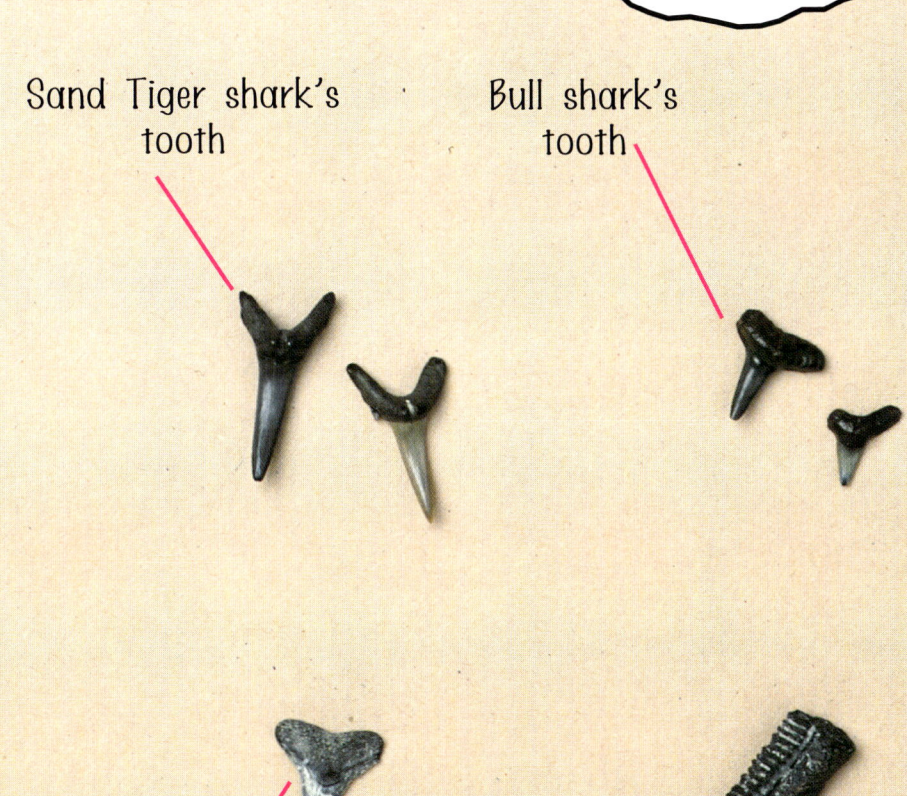

Sand Tiger shark's tooth

Bull shark's tooth

Dusky shark's tooth

Stingray's mouthplate

Friday 10th August
Going home

At the end of the day we watched the sun go down. What a great holiday!

My holiday highlights

Things I liked
- going to the beach
- collecting sharks' teeth
- my manatee souvenir
- Shamu the orca
- playing with Lydia

Things I did not like
- going shopping
- driving in the car for ages
- mosquitoes!
- dangerous marine life
- cutting my foot
- Lydia in a bad mood

Make your own holiday diary

Why don't you write a diary on your next holiday or day out?

Write about
- the places you visit
- the things you see
- the things you do
- special things and ordinary things
- things you like and do not like
- things that you learn

Ordinary things

Special things

These questions will help you to write your diary.

- **Who?**
  Write about who is with you.

- **Where?**
  Write about where you go.
  (You could draw a map.)

- **What?**
  Write about what happens.
  (You could take photographs or draw pictures of what you see.)

- **When?**
  Write the date when each thing happens.

Did you know that some people write in their diary every day?

Index

airport 4
beach 8–9, 10, 18, 21
diary 22–23,
dolphins 13
flags 9
Florida 5, 6
fort 8
fossils 19
guide book 19
highlights 21
hotel 6–7, 16
lifeguard 9
manatee 6, 13, 21
orca 14, 21
Orlando 12
restaurant 17
Sarasota 6
sharks 13
sharks' teeth 18–19, 21
shells 10
stingrays 9, 13
swimming pool 6–7, 16
trainers 14–15
Venice Beach 18